enjoy the
adventure!

This book is dedicated to my wife.
You mean the world to me!

ISBN # 978-0-692-34710-2

Printed in China

Ordering Information:
www.TheAdventuresoftheStarfishFamily.com

Meet the Starfish Family

 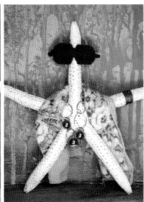 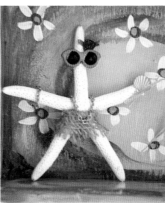  

Sunnee
Dad

Sandee
Mom

Shellee
Daughter

Reef
Son

Rocco
Son

My name is Rocco and
I am a Starfish you see.
This is the story of
me and my family.

1.

My parents, Sunnee and
Sandee, decided to wed
on a beautiful shore.
A sunny day in Destin
they couldn't ask for more.

3.

My sister Shellee
loves to be outside,
she rides her scooter
far and wide.

5.

This is my brother Reef,
there is one thing he craves.
That's being in the water,
and catching big waves.

Now that you've met
me and my family,
lets go on adventures
fun I guarantee!

9.   ★ Fun Fact #1: There are over 2,000 different kinds of starfish.

You can grab your
family hand in hand,
and have a beach
party in the sand.

11.

There is much
to be explored,
so jump on your
paddle board.

13.

Go out dancing and
listen to great music,
Electric
and
Acoustic.

15.

Need a change
from being poolside,
enjoy a beach side
bike ride.

17. ★ Fun Fact #2: Starfish are also called Sea Stars.

Grab a shovel
in your hand,
and bury a buddy
in the sand.

19.

If you are bored and
things are too quiet,
get to the beach and
act like a pirate.

21.

If tennis is
your favorite sport,
spend some time
on the courts.

23.

There is so much
to do in the sun,
including
Mardi Gras fun!

★ Fun Fact #3: Not all starfish have 5 arms.
Some have 10, 20 even 30 arms.

25.

Always something
to celebrate,
perfect for making
birthdays great!

27.

The beach is a great
place to come together
and create friendships
that will last forever.

29.

The whole family
will think its a treat,
whether fishing
from a boat or
from the beach.

Inhale...Exhale...
PARASAIL!

33. ★ Fun Fact #4: Starfish can live up to 35 years.

If you are wanting to be
on the golf course all day,
there are lots of choices
where to play.

35.

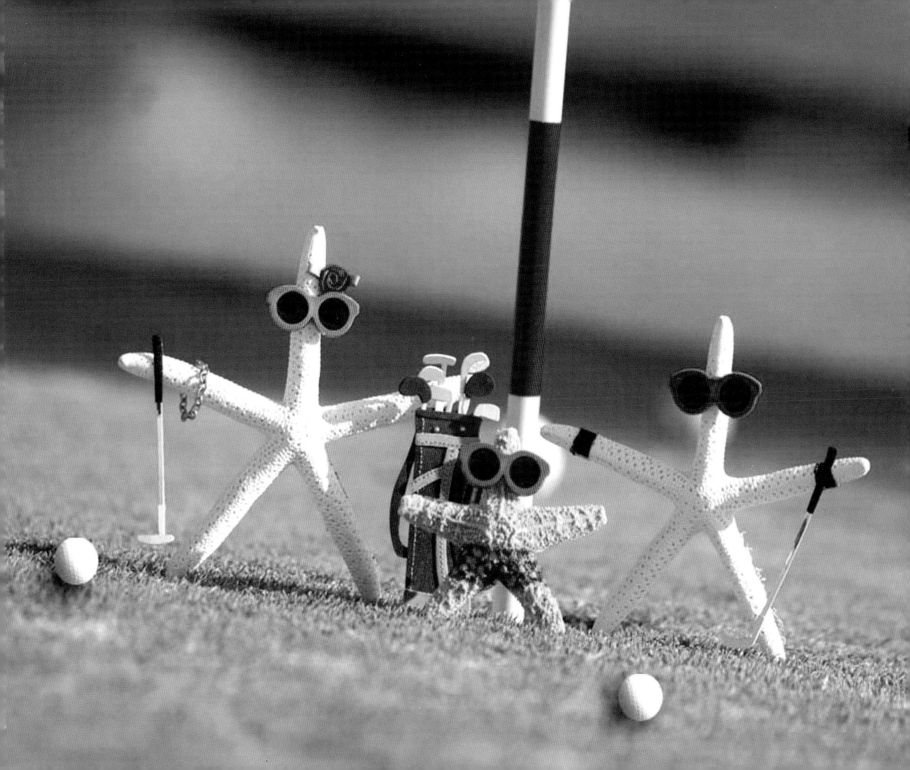

If a sandcastle
is not in the plan,
get creative and
build a snowman.

37.

Get inspired by the
amazing beach views,
take an art class to
learn something new.

39.

One thing you
will not regret,
is slowing down
and watching sunsets.

41.   ⭐ Fun Fact #5: Starfish can regenerate a lost arm.

Our family reunions are
great, everyone has fun.
Destin is the best choice
for family fun in the sun.

It is time for us to move on,
more fun we guarantee.
Because these are
The Adventures of the
Starfish Family!

43.

The Map of Adventures

CHOCTAWATCHEE BAY

293   331

NAVARRE   FT. WALTON BEACH   DESTIN   MIRAMAR BEACH

98   98

30A   393   83   283   395

GULF PLACE
BLUE MTN BEACH
GRAYTON BEACH
WATERCOLOR

SEASIDE
SEAGROVE BEACH
ROSEMARY BEACH

← Pensacola

Panama City Beach →

FUN TO DO:
Surfing Navarre Beach
Parasailing at Okaloosa Island
Fishing out of Destin Harbor
Weddings in Crystal Beach

Tennis in Miramar Beach
Golfing at Sandestin
Live Music at Gulf Place
Paddleboarding Watercolor
Bicycle Rides in Seaside

John Hollan is a photographer and artist born in Wynne, Arkansas. He graduated from the University of Arkansas in Fayetteville with a business degree and soon after decided to pursue a career in photography. John Hollan Photography was founded in 1995 and he has photographed countless families, locations and events over the years. He and his wife moved to the beach in 2005 and in 2008 John found his home as one of the Artists at Gulf Place on Scenic 30A in Santa Rosa Beach. John created and photographed the starfish wedding and the response was great. So great that today the Starfish Family is growing, adventures continue and they even have their own book.